THE BEST IRISH SONGS IN THE WORLD...EVER

A Bunch Of Thyme 2
After All These Years 4
An Old Irish Lady (Sweet Mother Of Mine) 7
Back In Old Ireland 10
The Black Velvet Band 13
Danny Boy (Londonderry Air) 16
Dear Old Donegal 20
Did Your Mother Come From Ireland 24
The Fields Of Athenry 27
Forty Shades Of Green 30
Galway Bay 34
How Can You Buy Killarney 32
I'll Take You Home Again Kathleen 37
If You Ever Go To Ireland 44
If You're Irish Come Into The Parlour 40
Ireland Must Be Heaven (For My Mother Came From There) 47
Irish Eyes 50
The Irish Rover 52
It's A Great Day For The Irish 54
It's A Long Way To Tipperary 58
Molly Malone 60
The Mountains Of Mourne 62
My Wild Irish Rose 68
Patsy Fagan (The Dacent Irish Boy) 74
Rose Of Tralee 72
The Spinning Wheel 77
The Town I Loved So Well 80
When Irish Eyes Are Smiling 84
Whistling Gypsy (The Gypsy Rover) 88
The Wild Colonial Boy 90
With My Shillelagh Under My Arm 93

This publication is not authorised for sale in the United States of America and/or Canada.

WISE PUBLICATIONS
London/New York/Paris/Sydney/Copenhagen/Madrid

A Bunch Of Thyme

Traditional

© Copyright 1998 Dorsey Brothers Music Limited, 8/9 Frith Street, London W1.
All Rights Reserved. International Copyright Secured.

1. Come all you maid-ens young and fair, _____ all you that are bloom-ing in your prime. _____

Verse 2:
For thyme it is a precious thing
And thyme brings all things to my mind.
Thyme, with all its labours
Along with all its joys
Thyme brings all things to my mind.

Verse 3:
Once she had a bunch of thyme,
She thought it never would decay,
Then came a lusty sailor
Who chanced to pass her way.
He stole her bunch of thyme away.

Verse 4:
The sailor gave to her a rose,
A rose that never would decay,
He gave it to her
To keep her reminded
Of when he stole her thyme away.

Verse 5:
Repeat Verse 1

Verse 6:
For thyme it is a precious thing
And thyme brings all things to my mind.
Thyme, with all its labours
Along with all its joys
Thyme brings all things to an end.

After All These Years

Words & Music by Barbara Coleman & Ollie Kennedy
© Copyright Asdee Music, Dublin, Ireland.
All Rights Reserved. International Copyright Secured.

1. My dar-ling come to me sit you down eas-i-ly
(Verse 2 see block lyric)
and rest a-while near the soft fire light, cold as the

night. But warm is my heart with pride having you by my side you're still my guiding light after all these years.

Your soft as-sur-ing ways, the rock I lean on saw me through my dark-est days when all hope had gone. You're still the

Verse 2:
Time from me passes on and I'm growing old
A lifetime nearly gone I cannot unfold
Nights dark and cold.
But warm is your hand in mine
Feeble with ageless time
The light of love still shines
After all these years.

An Old Irish Lady (Sweet Mother Of Mine)

Words & Music by John Watson & Muriel Watson

© Copyright 1935 Reproduced by permission of Keith Prowse Music Publishing Company Limited, 127 Charing Cross Road, London WC2.
All Rights Reserved. International Copyright Secured.

Moderato (with expression)

Sure I'll sing you a song of a lady so true, who cap-tured my heart long a-go; tho' I've not seen her for

know that she'll wel-come me home once a-gain, I'll see her dear eyes all a-shine. Deep in her heart there's a

G Am7 D♯7 G A7 A9 A7(♭9) A7/D D7
CHORUS
ma - ny a day, she'll be wait - ing I know.
place just for me, filled with a love that's di - vine.
There's an
mf
p
G G7 C G Cm/G
old Ir - ish la - dy I'm wish - ful to see, she's a smile in her
mp
G A7 Dsus4 D7 G G7
eyes worth a mil - lion to me; tho' I've seen ma - ny col - leens there's
mf
p
mf
C C♯dim G/D Cm6 G C6 C Cm6
none can com - pare to that old Ir - ish la - dy with sil - ver - y
mp
mf

hair. There was ma-ny a time when she belt-ed me sore, tho' I knew in me heart I de-served it and more, still I love ev-'ry hair, ev-'ry wrin-kle so fine of that old Ir-ish la-dy, sweet moth-er of mine. There's an mine. Sure I mine.

Back In Old Ireland

Words by Eddie Gillanders & Pat Michael ♣ Music by Dennis Cummings & Douglas Cummings

© Copyright 1951 Campbell Connelly & Company Limited, 8/9 Frith Street, London W1.
All Rights Reserved. International Copyright Secured

Andante

It's many years since I left Erin's shore, leaving my dear ones behind. Now I'm going back to the ones I adore, there's still a few things on my mind.

CHORUS

Back in old Ireland, is the Shannon still flowing? Do the mountains of Mourne still sweep down to the sea? Back in old Ireland are the shamrocks still growing? Do they still have a lady called

Mother Machree? Are the girls just as pretty? Are they still called colleens? And is Dublin's fair city the same as my dreams? If there's still a blarney and lakes called Killarney, Sure it's back in old Ireland that I long to be. be.

The Black Velvet Band

Irish Traditional

© Copyright 1998 Dorsey Brothers Music Limited, 8/9 Frith Street, London W1.
All Rights Reserved. International Copyright Secured.

1. As I went walking down Broadway, not intending to stay very long. I met with a frolicksome damsel as

13

B7 E
she came a trip-ping a - long. A watch she pulled out of her
A B7
pock - et and slipped it right in - to my hand. On the
E C♯m B7 E
fr4
ve - ry first day that I met her, bad luck to the black vel - vet band. Her
CHORUS E A
eyes they shone like dia - monds you'd think she was queen of the

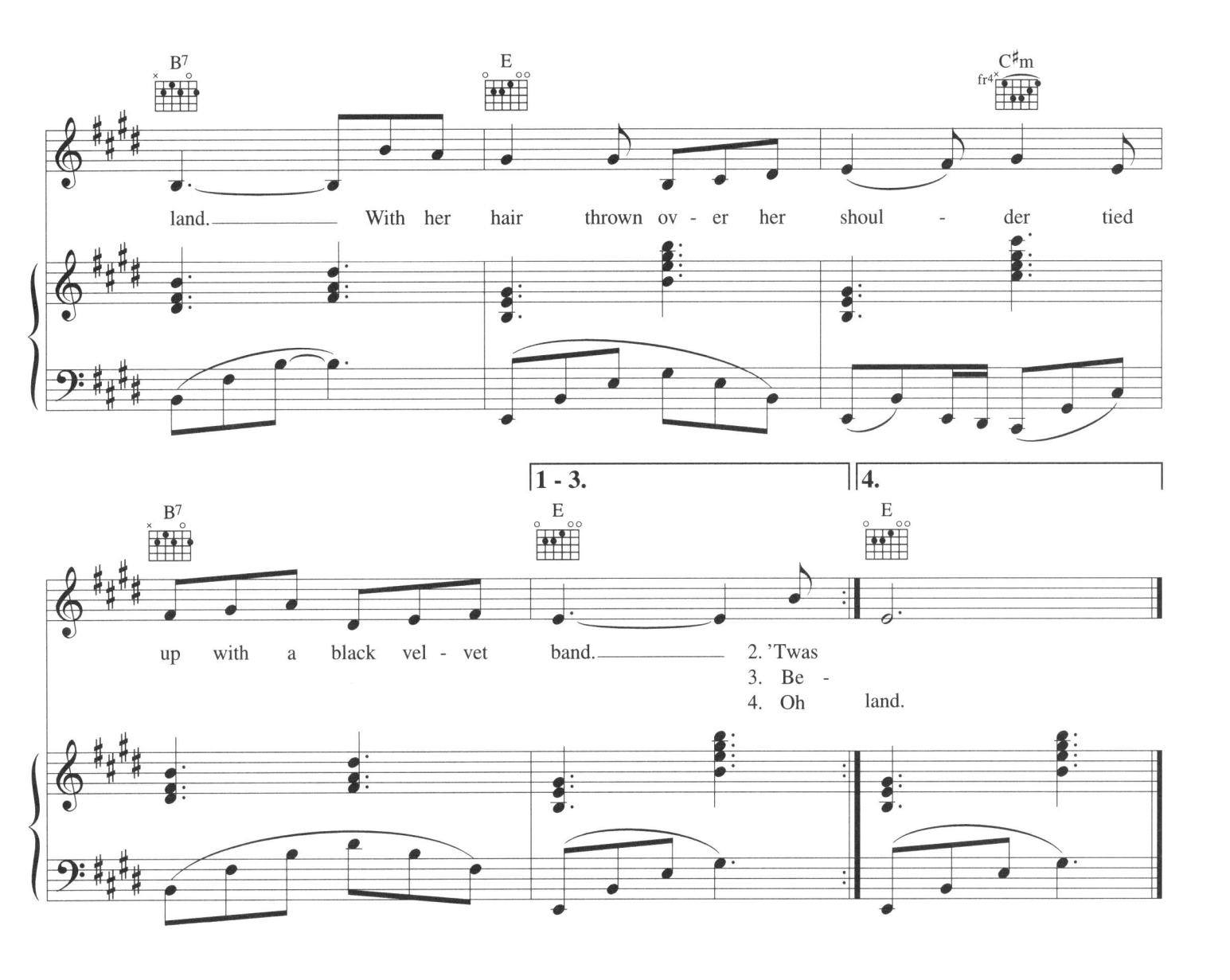

Verse 2:
'Twas in the town of Tralee an apprentice to trade I was bound
With a-plenty of bright amusement to see the days go round
Till misfortune and trouble came over me, which caused me to stray from my land,
Far away from my friends and relations, to fol-low the Black Velvet Band.

Verse 3:
Before the judge and the jury the both of us had to appear,
And a gentleman swore to the jewellery–the case against us was clear,
For seven years transportation right unto Van Dieman's Land
Far away from my friends and relations, to follow her Black Velvet Band.

Verse 4:
Oh all you brave young Irish lads, a warning take by me
Beware of the pretty young damsels that are knocking around in Tralee
They'll treat you to whiskey and porter, until you're unable to stand
And before you have time for to leave them, you are unto Van Dieman's Land.

Danny Boy (Londonderry Air)

Traditional Irish Melody ♣ Words by Fred E. Weatherly

© Copyright 1998 Dorsey Brothers Music Limited, 8/9 Frith Street, London W1.
All Rights Reserved. International Copyright Secured.

Andante

Oh, Danny Boy, / Oh, Ei-ly dear, the pipes, the pipes are call-ing from glen to glen, and down the moun-tain side, the sum-mer's

C C7 F6 G9 C Dm/F C C/G F/G
gone, and all the ros - es fall - ing, it's you, I, it's you I must go, and I you must
C G7 C F/C G/C C F/C C F/G G7
bide. But come ye I'll come back when sum-mer's in the mea - dow, or when the
mf
C/E F C Gsus4 G7 C C7 F6
val - ley's hushed and white with snow, it's and I'll you'll be here in sun-shine or in
C7 F D/A C/G G9 C C7
sha - dow, oh, Dan - ny Boy, oh, Dan - ny Boy, oh, Ei - ly dear, oh, Ei - ly dear, I love you so!

But when ye *Some-day, may* come, and *be, when* all the flow'rs are dy-ing, *if and* I am dead, as dead I well may be, ye'll come and find the place where I am ly-ing, and kneel and say an A-ve there for me; and I shall

18

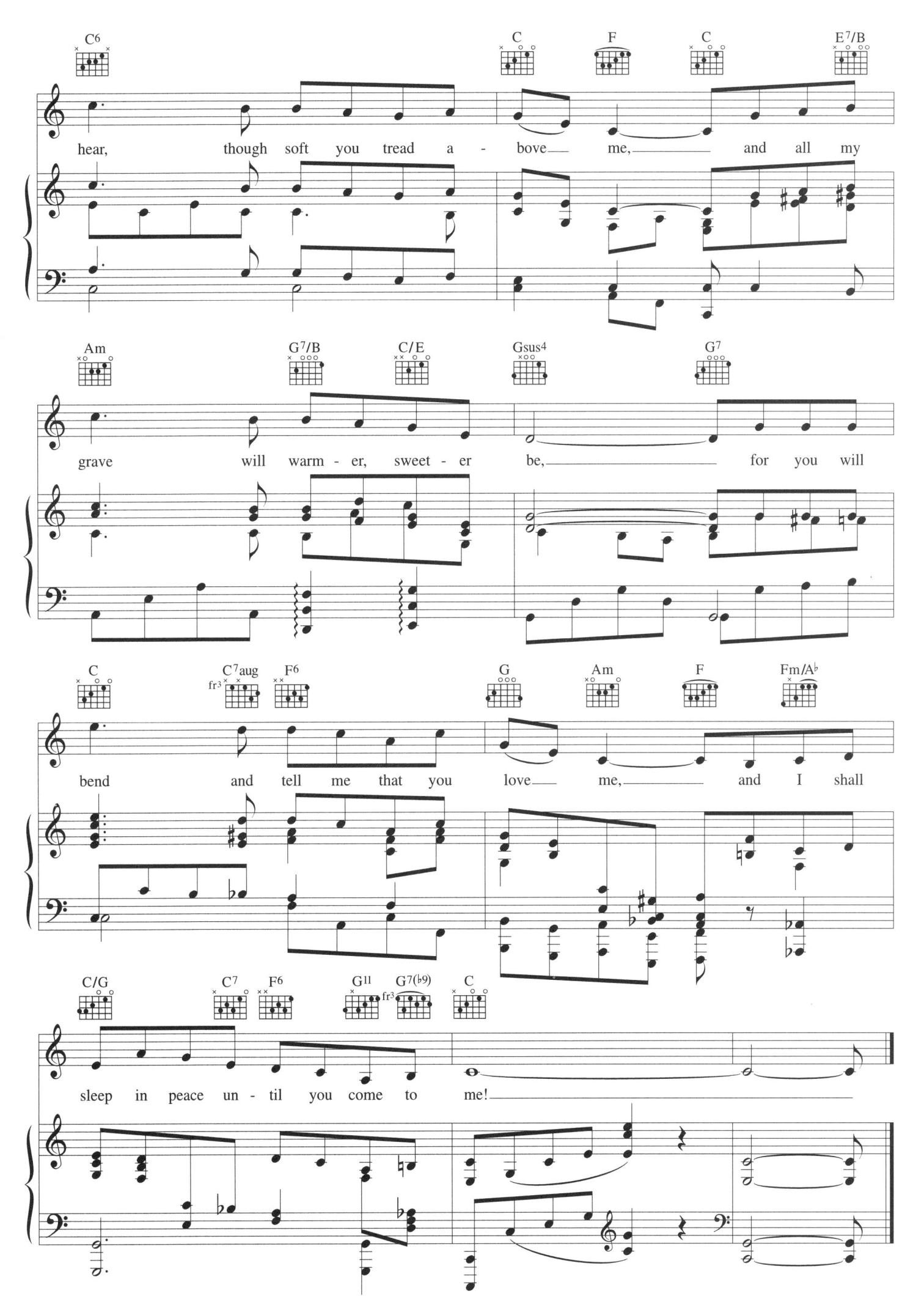

hear, though soft you tread a-bove me, and all my grave will warm-er, sweet-er be, for you will bend and tell me that you love me, and I shall sleep in peace un-til you come to me!

Dear Old Donegal

Words & Music by Steve Graham

© Copyright 1942 MCA Music (a division of MCA Incorporated, USA).
MCA Music Limited, 77 Fulham Palace Road, London W6 for the world (excluding North, South and Central America, Japan, Australasia and the Philippines).
All Rights Reserved. International Copyright Secured.

Moderately bright

VERSE

It seems like on-ly yes-ter-day I sailed from out of Cork, a wan-der-er from Er-in's isle, I land-ed in New York. There

give a par-ty when I go home, they'll come from near and far, they'll line the roads for miles and miles with Ir-ish jaunt-in' cars. The

E♭
A♭
E♭
was - n't a soul to greet me there, a stran - ger on your shore, but
spi - rits - 'll flow and we'll be gay, we'll fill your hearts with joy, the
A♭
A dim
E♭/B♭
C7
F7
B♭11
B♭7
E♭
Ir - ish luck was with me here and rich - es came ga - lore. And
pi - per'll play an Ir - ish reel to greet the Yan - kee boy. We'll
A♭
A dim
E♭/B♭
B♭/A♭
Gm7
Cm7
now that I'm go - in' back a - gain to dear old Er - in's isle, my
dance and sing the whole night long, such fun as nev - er seen, the
Gm
A♭
Gm
F7
B♭7sus4
B♭7
friends will meet me on the pier and greet me with a smile, their
lads be decked in cor - du - roy, the col - leens wear - in' green, there'll

fa - ces, sure, I've al - most for - got I've been so long a - way, _____ but me
be thou - sands there that I nev - er saw I've been so long a - way, _____ but me

moth - er will in - tro - duce them all and this to me will say. _____ } Shake
moth - er will in - tro - duce them all and this to me will say. _____ } Shake

CHORUS

hands with your Un - cle Mike, me boy, and here is your sis - ter Kate, _____ and

there's the girl you used to swing down by the gar - den gate. _____ Shake hands with all of the neigh-bours___ and kiss the col-leens all,___ you're as wel-come as the flow'rs in May to dear old Don-e-gal.___ They'll gal.___

Patter *(Optional) after 2nd Verse*

Meet Bran-i-gan, Fan-ni-gan, Mil-li-gan, Gil-li-gan, Duf-fy, McCuf-fy, Ma-la-chy, Ma-hone,
Mad-i-gan, Cad-i-gan, Lan-i-han, Flan-i-han, Fa-gan, O'-Ha-gan, O'-Hoo-li-han, Flynn,
Raf-er-ty, Laf-er-ty, Don-nel-ly, Con-nel-ly, Doo-ley, O'Hoo-ley, Mul-down-ey, Ma-lone. Guin-ness, McGuinn.
Shan-i-han, Man-i-han, Fo-gar-ty, Ho-gar-ty, Kel-ly, O'-Kel-ly, Mc-

Did Your Mother Come From Ireland

Words & Music by Michael Carr & Jimmy Kennedy
© Copyright 1936 Keith Prowse Music Publishing Company Limited, 127 Charing Cross Road, London WC2.
All Rights Reserved. International Copyright Secured.

Slowly

VERSE

Oh! I've never seen old Ireland o'er the ocean, tho' I've wished for the chance to greet it, in my mind I've always had a crazy notion, that I'd know a bit of Irish when I meet it. Did your

mother come from Ireland? 'Cos there's some-thing in you I-rish, will you tell me where you get those I-rish eyes? And be-fore she left Kil-lar-ney, did your moth-er kiss the blar-ney? 'Cos your lit-tle touch of brogue you can't dis-guise. Oh! I wouldn't be romancin', I can almost see you dancin' while the Kerry pipers play, Shure! And maybe we'll be sharin' in the shamrock you'll be wearin', on the next St. Patrick's Day. Did your mother come from Ireland? 'Cos there's something in you Irish, and that bit of Irish steals my heart away. Did your way.

The Fields Of Athenry

Words & Music by Pete St. John
© Copyright Celtic Music/Saint Music, Dublin, Ireland.
All Rights Reserved. International Copyright Secured.

By a lone-ly pri-son wall I heard a young girl call-ing Mich-ael they have tak-en you a-

-way.___ For you stole Tre-vel-yn's corn so the young might see the morn now a pri-son ship lies wait-ing in the bay.___ Low lie the fields of Ath-en--ry where once we watched the small free birds fly.___ Our

Verse 2:
By a lonely prison wall
I heard a young man calling
Mary nothing matters when you're free
Against the famine and the crown
I rebelled they ran me down.
Chorus

Verse 3:
By a lonely harbour wall
She watched the last star falling
As the prison ship sailed out against the sky
Sure she'll live and hope and pray
For her love of Botany Bay
It's so lovely round the fields of Athenry.
Chorus

Forty Shades Of Green

Words & Music by Johnny Cash

© Copyright 1961 by Southwind Music Incorporated, USA.
Carlin Music Corporation, Iron Bridge House, 3 Bridge Approach, London NW1 for the United
Kingdom, British Commonwealth (excluding Canada and Australasia), Israel and the Republic of Ireland.
All Rights Reserved. International Copyright Secured.

Moderately with feeling

1. I close my eyes and picture the em-'rald of the sea, from the fishing boats at Dingle to the shores of Dunadee, I miss the river Shannon, and the

wish that I could spend an hour at Dublin's churning surf, I'd love to watch the farmer drain the bogs and spade the turf, to see again the thatching of the

folks at Skip-pa-ree, the Moor-lands and the Mid-lands with their for-ty shades of green. But
straw the wo-men glean, I'd walk from Cork to Liarn to see the for-ty shades of green.

most of all I miss a girl in Tip-pe-ra-ry Town, and most of all I miss her lips, as

soft as ei-der-down, a-gain I want to see and do the things we've done and seen, where the

breeze is sweet as Shal-i-mar and there's for-ty shades of green. 2. I green.

How Can You Buy Killarney

Words & Music by Freddie Grant, Gerald Morrison, Hamilton Kennedy & Ted Steels

© Copyright 1948 Reproduced by permission of Peter Maurice Music Company Limited, 127 Charing Cross Road, London WC2.
All Rights Reserved. International Copyright Secured.

Slowly and expressively

1. An American landed on Erin's green isle, he gazed at Killarney with rapturous smile, "How can I buy it?" He said to his guide, "I'll tell you how," with a smile he replied.

2. Such a wonderful landscape you never have seen, a jewel so rare t'would befit any queen, pride of old Erin, a joy to behold, heaven on earth, far more precious than gold.

How can you buy all the stars in the skies? How can you buy two blue Irish eyes? How can you purchase a fond mother's sighs? How can you buy Killarney? Nature bestowed all her gifts with a smile, the em-'rald, the sham-rock, the blarney. When you can buy all these wonderful things, then you can buy Killarney. larney.

Galway Bay

Words & Music by Dr Arthur Colahan

© Copyright 1947 by Box & Cox Publications Limited. Published by permission of McCullough Pigott Limited, 11/13 Suffolk Street, Dublin, Eire.
All Rights Reserved. International Copyright Secured.

Moderato

If you ever go a-cross the sea to Ire-land, then may-be at the clos-ing of your day, you will sit and watch the moon rise ov-er Clad-dagh, and

breez-es blow-ing o'er the seas from Ire-land, are per-fumed by the heath-er as they blow, and the wo-men in the up-lands dig-gin' pra-ties, speak a

34

see the sun go down on Galway Bay. Just to
language that the strangers do not know. For the

hear again the ripple of the trout stream, the women in the meadows making
strangers came and tried to teach us their way, they scorned us just for being what we

hay, and to sit beside a turf fire in the
are, but they might as well go chasing after

cabin, and watch the barefoot Gossoons at their play. For the
moonbeams, or light a penny candle from a

2.
F
F9/A
Gm7
Gm6
C
fr3
star. And if there is going to be a life here - af - ter, and
C7
F
some - how I am sure there's going to be, I will
F9
D7
G7
ask my God to let me make my hea - ven, in
C7
C9
C13
fr2
F
B♭6/F
F
that dear land a - cross the I - rish sea.

I'll Take You Home Again Kathleen

Words & Music by Thomas P. Westendorf

© Copyright 1998 Dorsey Brothers Music Limited, 8/9 Frith Street, London W1.
All Rights Reserved. International Copyright Secured.

Andante con espressione

I'll take you home a-gain, Kath-leen, a-cross the o-cean wild and wide, to where your heart has ev-er been, since first you were my bonny bride, the roses all have left your cheek, I've watched them fade away and die; your voice is sad when-e'er you speak, and

C/G
G7
C
C7
tears be - dim your lov - ing eyes. Oh,
F
C7
F
I will take you back, Kath - leen, to
C7
F
B♭
where your heart will know no pain, and when the fields are fresh and
Bdim
F/C
C7
F
green, I'll take you to your home a - gain.

If You're Irish Come Into The Parlour

Words & Music by Shaun Glenville & Frank Miller

© Copyright 1920 B. Feldman & Company Limited, 127 Charing Cross Road, London WC2.
All Rights Reserved. International Copyright Secured.

In sweet Lim-'rick Town, they say,_____ lived a chap named Pat-rick John Mol-loy,_____
loved the girl he wed,_____ but he could not stand his Ma-in-law,_____

40

once he sailed to U. S. A., his
once with joy he turned quite red, when
luck in fo-reign parts he thought he'd try. Now he's made his
she got in-to trou-ble through her jaw. Six po-lice they
name, and is a weal-thy man, he put a bit a-way for a rain-y
had to take her to the court, she was in-formed a month she would have to
day; so if you gaze up-on the house of Pat-rick
do, so Pat-rick quick-ly wrote up to the Judge, a

John,____ you'll find a no-tice that goes on to say:____ If you're
note,____ ex-plain-ing, Sir, I'm much o-bliged to you!____

I-rish____ come in-to the par - - lour, there's a wel-come
there for you;____ if your name is
Tim-o-thy or Pat,____ so long as you come from Ire-land, there's a wel-come on the

mat. If you come from the moun-tains of Mourne, or Kil-lar-ney's lakes so blue, we'll sing you a song and we'll make a fuss, who-ev-er you are, you are one of us, if you're I-rish, this is the place for you! If you're you! Pat-rick

If You Ever Go To Ireland

Words & Music by Art Noel

© Copyright 1943 Cinephonic Music Company Limited, 8/9 Frith Street, London W1.
All Rights Reserved. International Copyright Secured.

Moderato

Will you par-don me stran-ger, I know you're from Ire-land, Ire-land my home-land, the green em-'rald Isle. Sure I'm think-ing that one day you'll go back to

Ireland, if you do, can I say these few words with a smile. If you ever go to Ireland, will you take this message for me to a sweet old Irish lady, sure she's sweet as an angel can be.

You will find a white house where the green shamrock grows, where the mountains sweep down to the sea, if you ever go to Ireland, will you kiss my old mother for me.

rit. e cresc.

f rall. accel.

Ireland Must Be Heaven
(For My Mother Came From There)

Words & Music by Joseph McCarthy, Howard Johnson & Fred Fisher

© Copyright 1916 EMI Feist Catalog Incorporated, USA.
Worldwide print rights controlled by Warner Bros. Publications Incorporated/IMP Limited.
All Rights Reserved. International Copyright Secured.

Andante moderato

1. I've oft-en heard my dad-dy speak of Ire-land's lakes and dells, the place must be like Hea-ven, if it's half like what he tells; there's

pic-tured in my fond-est dreams old Ire-land's vales and rills, I see a stair-way to the sky, formed by her ver-dant hills; each

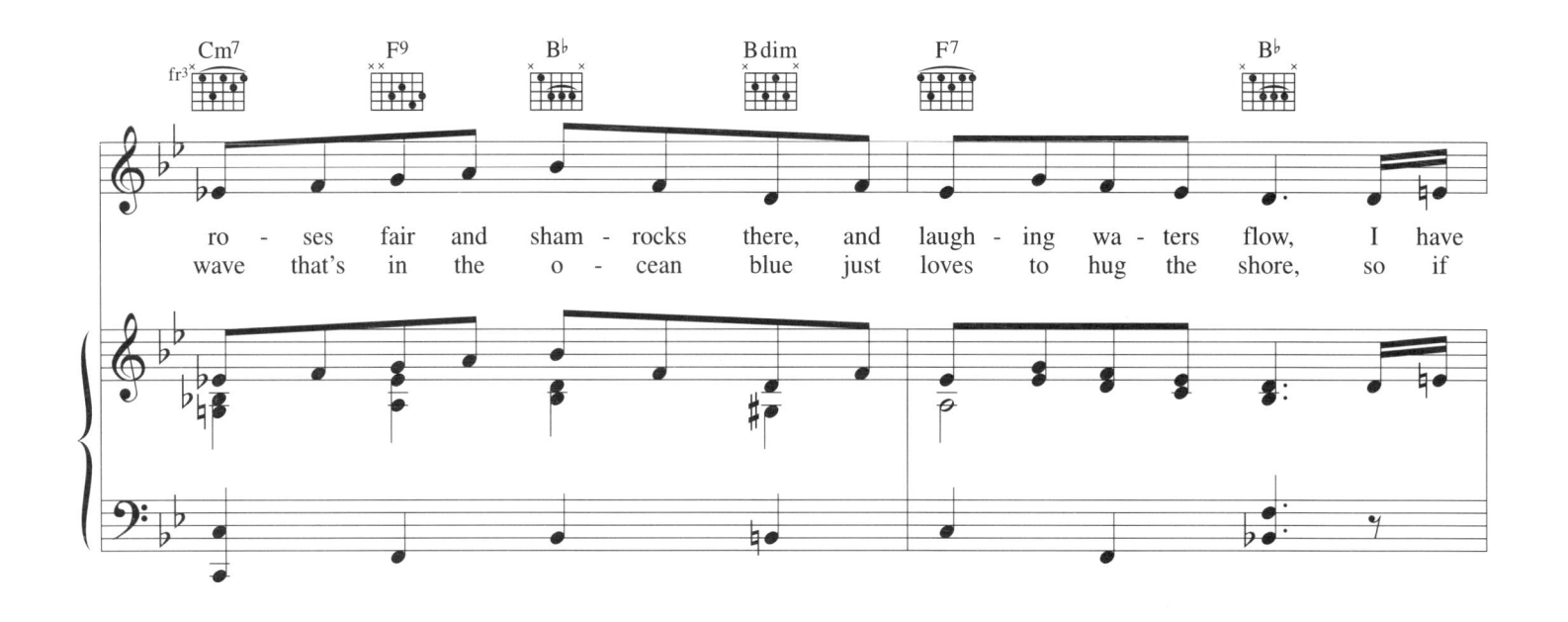

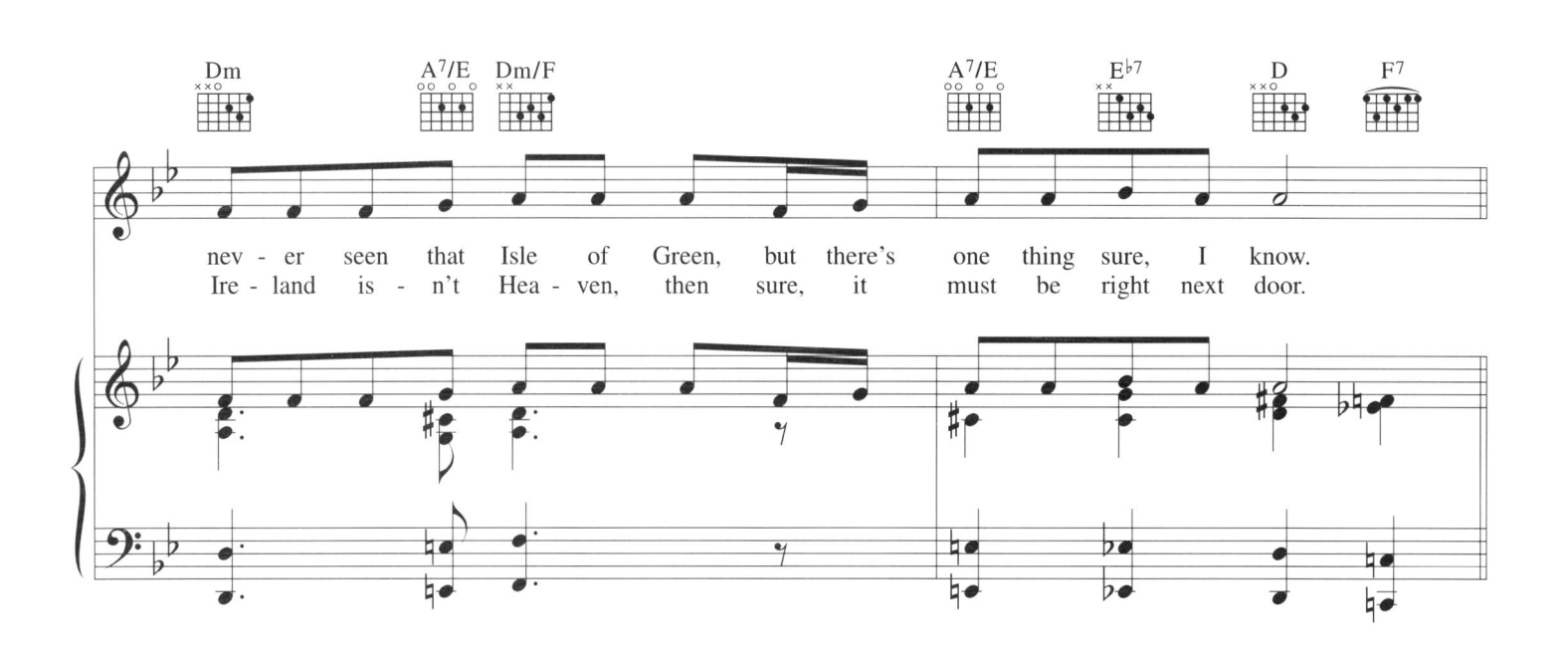

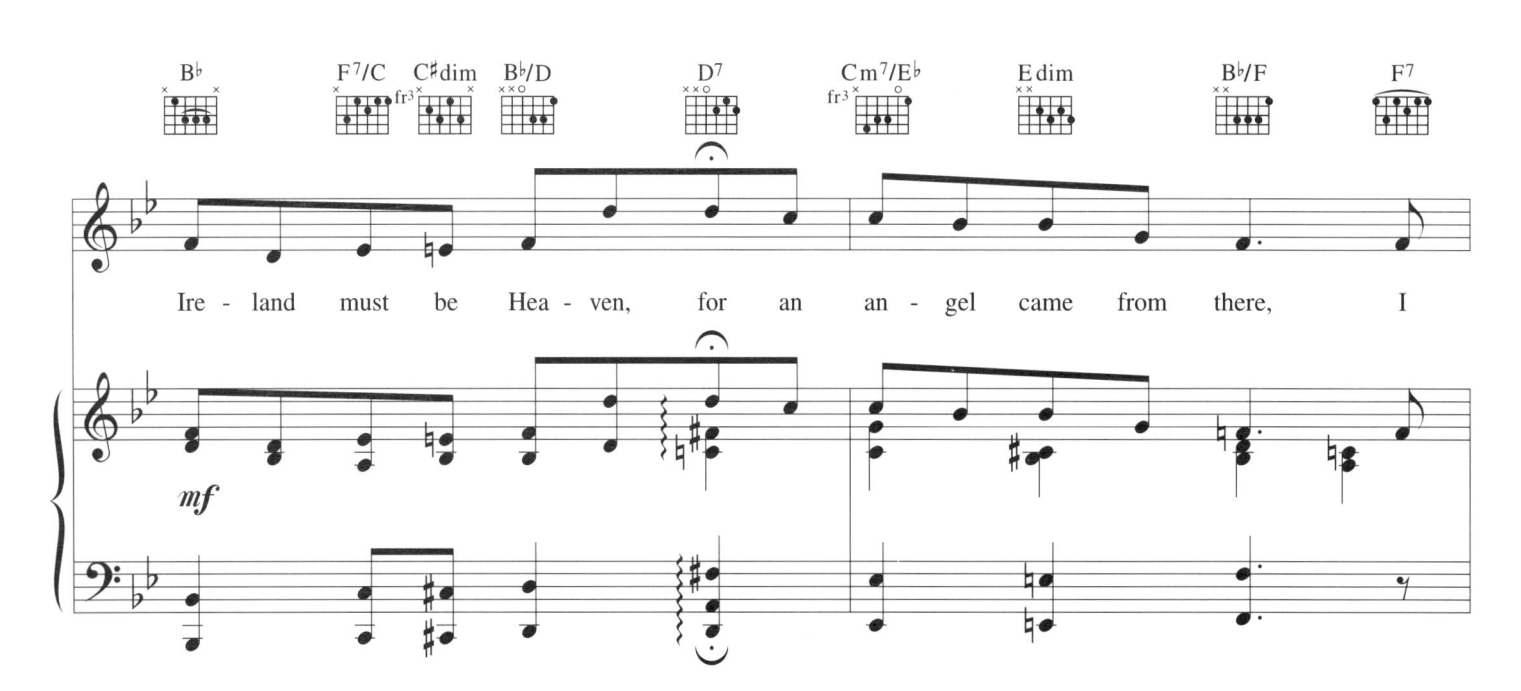

ro - ses fair and sham - rocks there, and laugh - ing wa - ters flow, I have
wave that's in the o - cean blue just loves to hug the shore, so if

nev - er seen that Isle of Green, but there's one thing sure, I know.
Ire - land is - n't Hea - ven, then sure, it must be right next door.

Ire - land must be Hea - ven, for an an - gel came from there, I never knew a living soul one half as sweet or fair, for her eyes are like the star-light, and the white clouds match her hair, sure Ireland must be Heaven, for my mother came from there. 2. I've

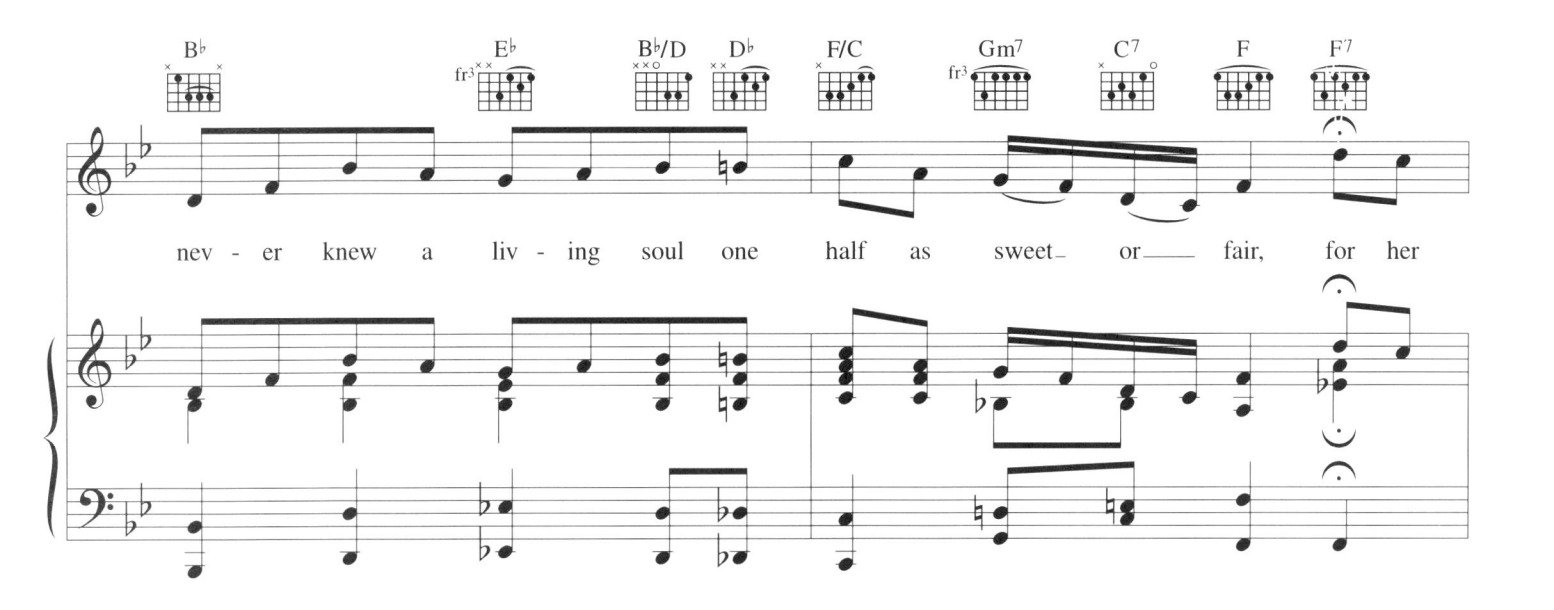

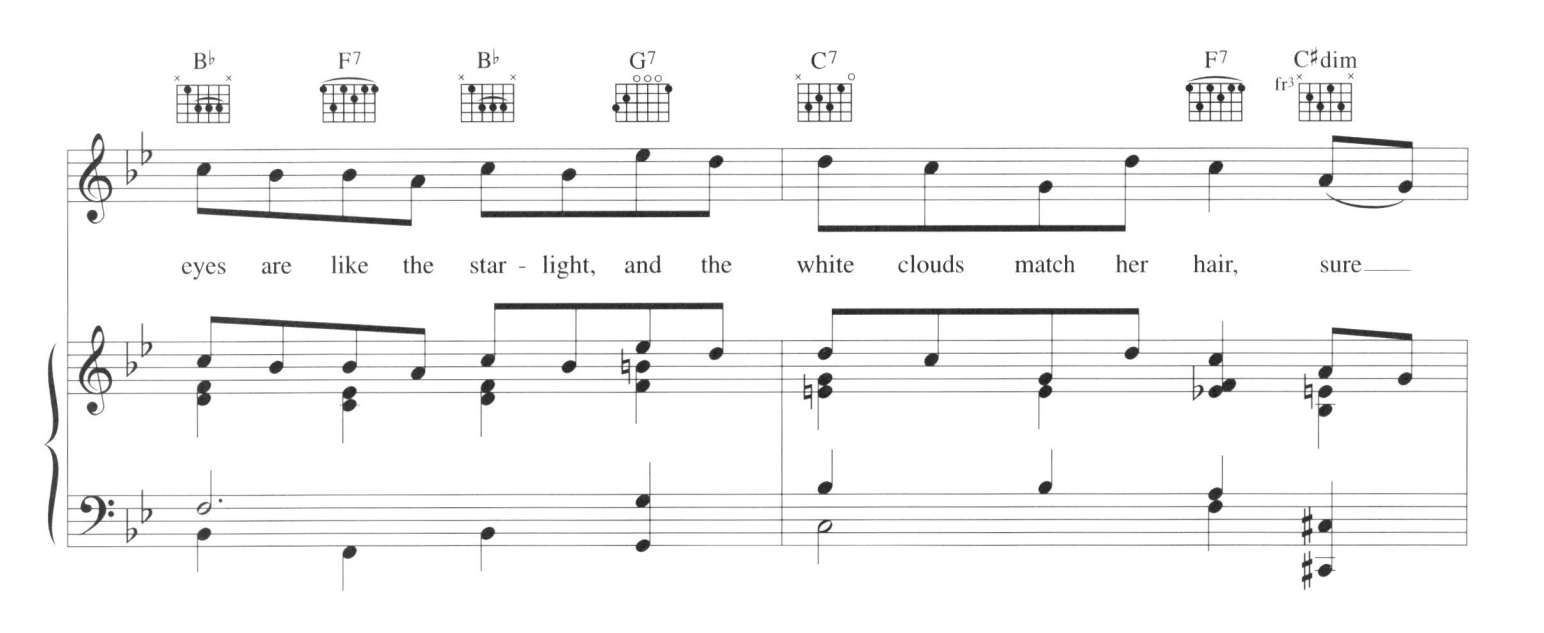

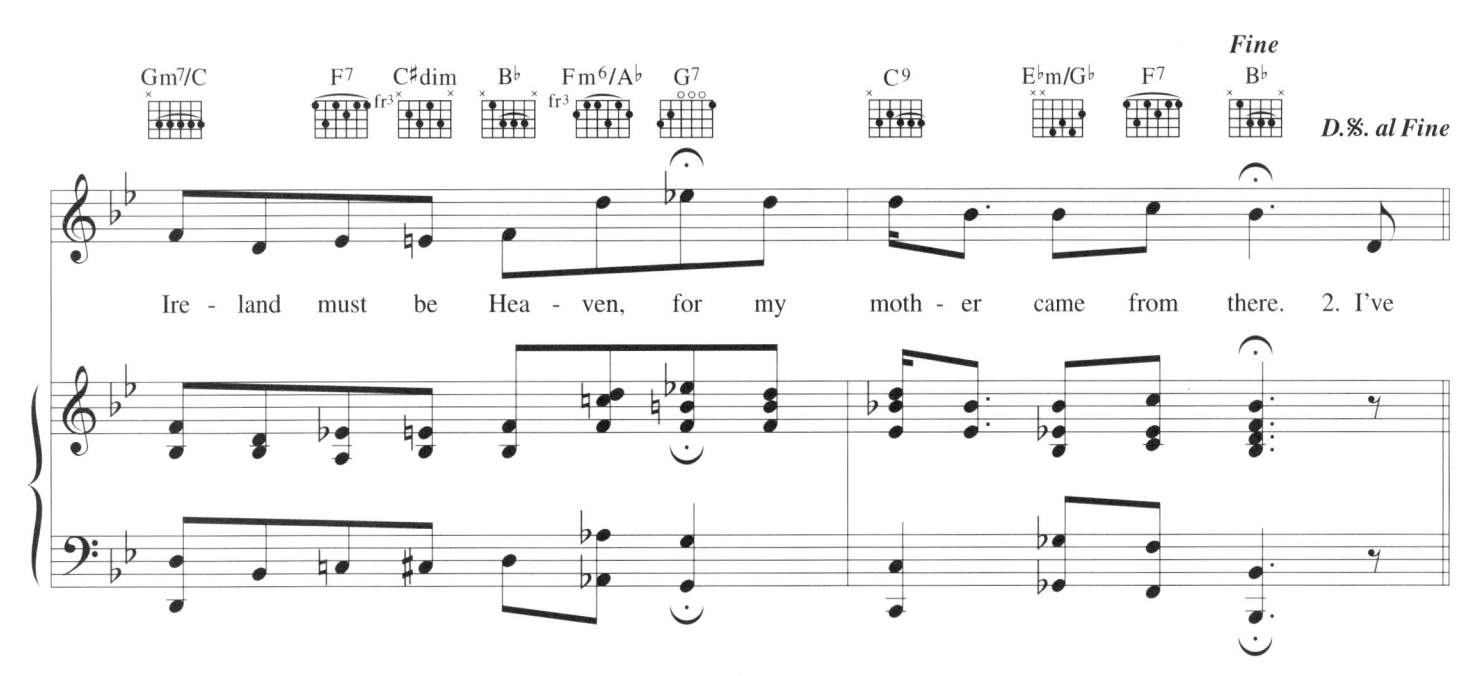

Irish Eyes

Words & Music by Hank Locklin & George Carroll

© Copyright 1974 Sawgrass Music Publishing Incorporated, USA.
Acuff-Rose Opryland Music Limited, 129 Park Street, London W1.
All Rights Reserved. International Copyright Secured.

1. The moon-light on the Shan-non is a sight to see. The sun-light on Kil-lar-ney's lakes means home sweet home to me. Of na-ture's ma-ny bless-ings

(Verses 2, 3 & 4 see block lyric)

Verse 2:

To stroll again Antrim's Glens and see the waterfall
To sleep beneath the mystic hills in dear old Donegal
Or walk the shores of Eireann and hear the seagulls cry
But most of all to look into your lovely Irish eyes.

Verse 3:

To hear again those Shandon bells ringing heavenly
Beside the laughing waters of the lovely Lee
Or listen to the ocean and the wind that sighs
But most of all to see again your smiling Irish eyes.

Verse 4:

In dreams I see your angel face that aches my lonely heart
The memory when I told you we would have to part
I can't forget that morning when we said goodbye
I can't forget those teardrops in your Irish eyes.
I love you and I need you, my lovely Irish eyes.

The Irish Rover

Traditional

© Copyright 1998 Dorsey Brothers Music Limited, 8/9 Frith Street, London W1.
All Rights Reserved. International Copyright Secured.

1. In the year of our Lord eighteen hundred and six, we set sail from the coal quay of Cork, we were sailing away with a cargo of bricks, for the grand city hall in New York. We'd an elegant craft, it was

(Verses 2, 3 & 4 see block lyric)

52

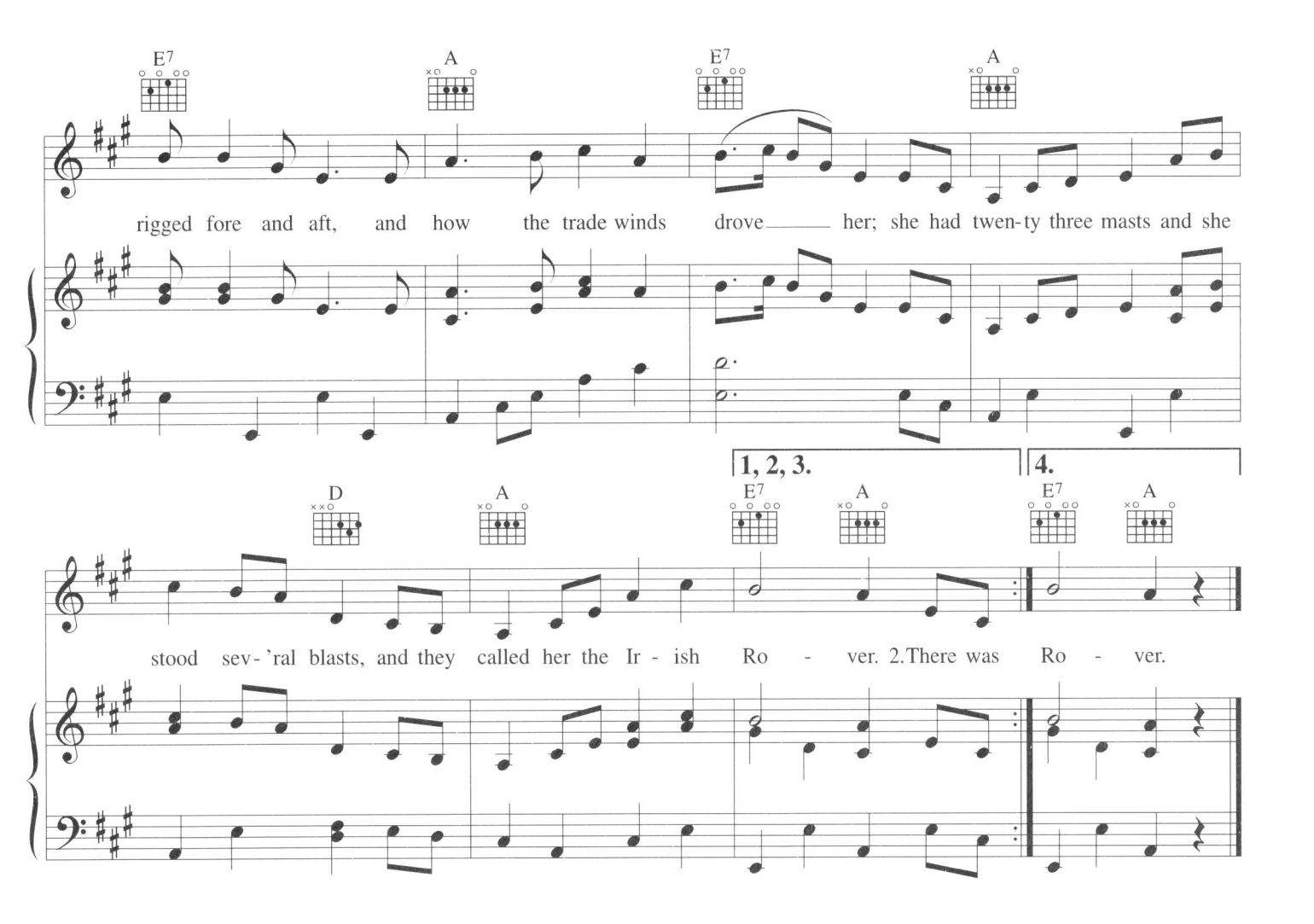

Verse 2:
There was Barney Magee, from the banks of the Lee
There was Hogan, from County Tyrone
There was Johnny McGurk, who was scared stiff of work
And a chap from Westmeath named Malone.
There was Slugger O'Toole, who was drunk as a rule
And fighting Bill Tracy from Dover.
And your man Mick McCann from the banks of the Bann
Was the skipper on the Irish Rover.

Verse 3:
We had one million bags of the best Sligo rags
We had two million barrels of bone
We had three million bales of old nanny goats' tails
We had four million barrels of stone.
We had five million hogs and six million dogs
And seven million barrels of porter.
We had eight million sides of old blind horses' hides
In the hold of the Irish Rover.

Verse 4:
We had sailed seven years when the measles broke out,
And our ship lost her way in a fog
And the whole of the crew was reduced down to two
'Twas myself and the captain's old dog.
Then the ship struck a rock, O Lord, what a shock
And nearly tumbled over
Turned nine times around, then the poor old dog was drowned.
I'm the last of the Irish Rover.

It's A Great Day For The Irish

Words & Music by Roger Edens

© Copyright 1940 EMI Catalogue Partnership & EMI Feist Catalog Incorporated, USA.
Worldwide print rights controlled by Warner Bros. Publications Incorporated/IMP Limited.
All Rights Reserved. International Copyright Secured.

Moderately–march tempo

Oh, I woke me up this morn-ing and I heard a joy-ful song from the throats of hap-py I-rish-men, a hun-dred thou-sand strong, Shure, it was the Hibernian Brigade lining up for to start the big parade, so I fetched me Sunday bonnet, and the flag I love so well, and I bought meself a shamrock just to wear in me lapel, don't you know that today's March Seventeen?

Cm D Gm6 D dim D7 G7 G dim G7
fr3
It's the day for the wear-ing of the Green! It's a
mp
C E♭dim G7 Dm7
great day for the Ir - ish, it's a great day
great day for the Ir - ish, it's a great day
G aug C Cmaj7 C6 G aug C C♯dim
fr3
for fair! The side-walks of New York are thick with
for fair! Be - gosh, there's not a Cop to stop a
Dm7 G7 Dm7 G7 C D7 G7 Dm7
Blar - ney, for shure you'd think New York was Old Kil - lar - ney!
raid - ing, be - gor - ra all the Cops are out pa - rad - ing!

G7 N.C. C E♭dim G7
It's a great day for the Sham - rock, for the
It's a great day for the Sham - rock, for the
Dm7 Gaug C C7 F
flags in full ar - ray, we're feel - ing so in -
flags in full ar - ray, and as we go a -
E7 Am D7 Fm6/A♭ C/G
spir - ish, shure be - cause for all the Ir - ish, it's a great,
swing - ing, ev - 'ry Ir - ish heart is sing - ing, it's a great,
cresc.
f
Dm7 G7 1. C Dm7 G7 N.C. 2. C F6 C
great day! It's a day!
great
mp
sfz

It's A Long Way To Tipperary

Words & Music by Jack Judge & Harry Williams

© Copyright 1912 B. Feldman & Company Limited, 127 Charing Cross Road, London WC2.
All Rights Reserved. International Copyright Secured.

C C7 Am C7/G F7 B♭
to the sweet - est girl I know! Good - bye
B♭7 E♭ D7
Pi - ca - dil - ly, fare - well, Leices - ter Square,
N.C. B♭ C♯dim B♭ Gm
it's a long, long way to Tip - per - ar - - - y, but my heart's
C7 F7 B♭
1. 2.
N.C.
right there! It's a there!

Molly Malone

Words & Music by George M. Cohan

© Copyright 1998 Dorsey Brothers Music Limited, 8/9 Frith Street, London W1.
All Rights Reserved. International Copyright Secured.

Slowly

In Dub-lin Ci-ty, where the girls they are so pret-ty, 'twas there I first met with sweet Mol-ly Ma-lone; she
She was a fish mon-ger and that was the won-der, her fa-ther and moth-er were fish mon-gers too; they
She died of the fa-ver, and noth-ing could save her, and that was the end of sweet Mol-ly Ma-lone; but her

drove a wheel-bar-row
drove wheel-bar-rows } thro' streets broad and nar-row, cry-ing,
ghost drives a bar-row

"Cock-les and mus-sels, a-live, all a-live!" A-

live, a-live-o! A-live, a-live-o! Cry-ing,

"Cock-les and mus-sels, a-live, all a-live!"

D.C.

The Mountains Of Mourne

Words & Music by Percy French & H. Collison
© Copyright 1998 Dorsey Brothers Music Limited, 8/9 Frith Street, London W1.
All Rights Reserved. International Copyright Secured.

Andante

Ma - ry! This Lon - don's a won - der - ful sight, wid the peo - ple here
lieve that, when writ - in', a wish you ex - pressed, as to how the fine

62

workin' by day and by night; they don't sow po- ta- toes, nor bar- ley, nor
la- dies in Lon- don were dressed. Well, if you'll be- lieve me, when axed to a

wheat, but there's gangs o' them dig- gin' for gold in the street; at
ball, faith they don't wear a top to their dress- es at all. Oh, I've

least, when I axed them that's what I was told, so I just took a
seen them me- self, and you could not, in thrath, say if they were

hand at this dig- gin' for gold, but for all that I found there I
bound for a ball or a bath. Don't be start- in' them fash- ions now,

Em A7 D7 C9 D7 G9 G/D Am7/E G
might as well be
Ma - ry Ma - cree
where the Moun-tains o' Mourne sweep down to the sea.
poco rall.
G B7 D7/C C C♯dim G/D G6/D D7
mf
pp
G9 G Cm6 G G D7
poco rall.
2. I be -
3. I've seen Eng - land's King from the
(4.) - mem - ber young Pe - ter O'
Am C D7 G C
top of a bus, I nev - er knew him, tho' he means to know
Lough - lin, of course? Well, now he is here at the head o' the

G D7 D♯dim Em A7
us; and tho' by the Sax - on we once were op - pressed, still, I
force; I met him to - day, I was cross - in' the Strand, and he
C9 D7 C9 D7 G Am7 G D7
cheered, (God for - give me) I cheered wid the rest. And now that he's
stopped the whole street wid wan wave of his hand; and there we stood
pp
D7/F♯ G C6/9 G
vi - sit - ed Er - in's green shore, we'll be much bet - ter friends than we've
talk - in' of days that are gone, while the whole pop - u - la - tion of
mf
A9 fr6 A7 D7 G D7 Em
been here - to - fore, when we've got all we want we're as quiet as can
Lon - don looked on, but for all these great pow - ers he's wish - ful, like

A7 D7 C9 D7 G9 G Am7/E G
be, where the Moun - tains o' Mourne sweep down to the sea.
me, to be back where dark Mourne sweeps down to the sea.
poco rall.
a tempo
B7 D7/C C C♯dim G6 G
mf
pp
G6 D7 G9 G Cm6 G G B7
4. You re -
5. There's beau - ti - ful girls here,
poco rall.
mp a tempo
B7/C C A7 G/D Am7 D7 C G C6 G
oh! niv - er mind! Wid beau - ti - ful shapes na - ture niv - er de - signed, and

lovely complexions all roses and crame, but O'-Lough-lin re-marked wid re-gard to the same; "That if at those ro-ses you ven-ture to sip, the co-lours might all come a-way on your lip. So I'll wait for the wild rose that's wait-in' for me where the Moun-tains o' Mourne sweep down to the sea."

My Wild Irish Rose

Words & Music by Chauncey Olcott

© Copyright 1899 M. Witmark & Sons, USA.
B. Feldman & Company Limited, 127 Charing Cross Road, London WC2.
All Rights Reserved. International Copyright Secured.

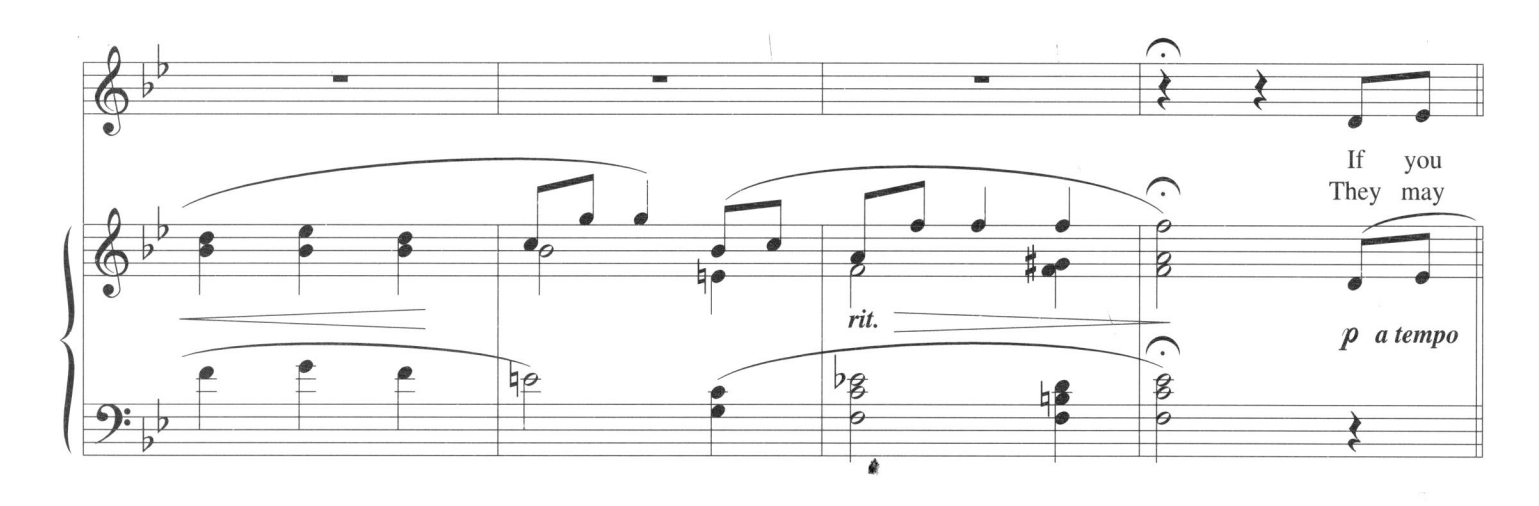

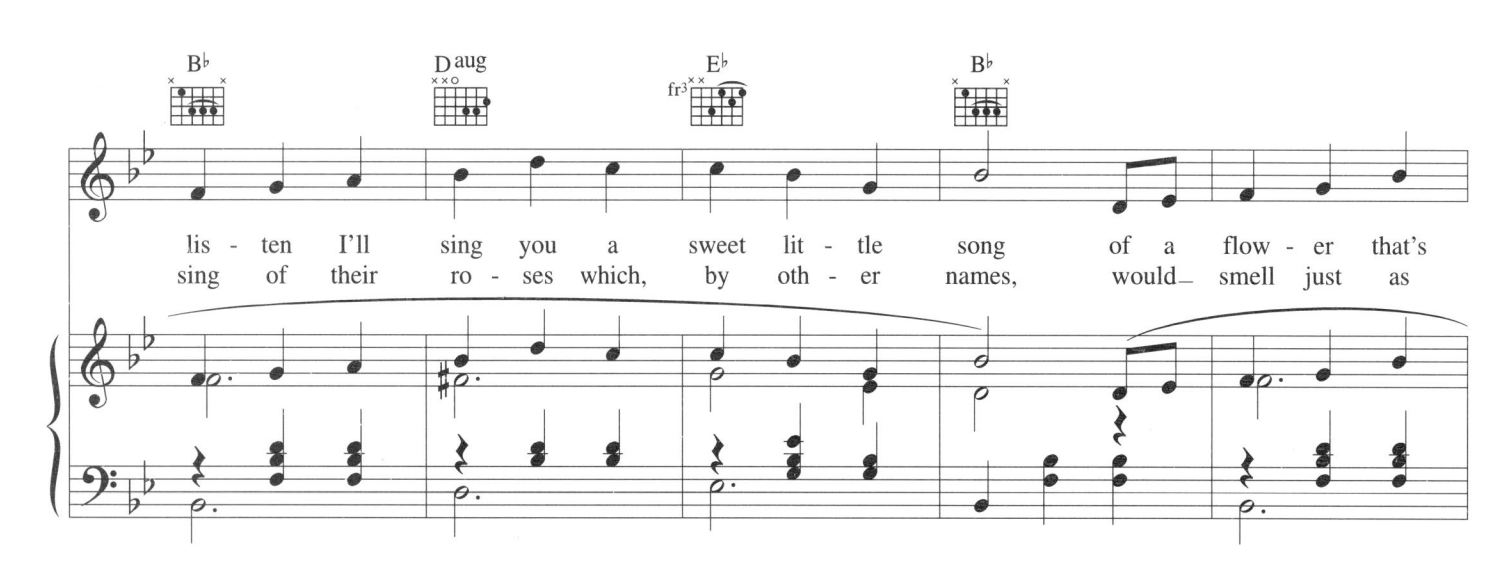

Lyrics:

If you listen I'll sing you a sweet little song of a flower that's
They may sing of their roses which, by other names, would smell just as

now drooped and dead, ___ yet dear-er to me, yes, than
sweet-ly, they say, ___ but I know that my Rose would

all of its mates, tho' each holds a-loft its proud head. ___
nev-er con-sent to have that sweet name tak-en a-way. ___

'Twas giv-en to me by a girl that I know, since we've
Her glanc-es are shy when-e'er I pass by, since the

met, faith, I've known no re-pose, ___ she is dear-er by
bow-er, where my true love grows; ___ and my one wish has

69

far than the world's bright-est star, and I call her my wild Irish
been that some day I may win the heart of my wild Irish

Rose. ⎫
Rose. ⎭ My wild Ir - ish Rose, the sweet-est flower that grows, you may

search ev-'ry-where but none can com-pare with my wild

Ir-ish Rose. My wild Ir-ish Rose, the dear-est flower that grows and some day for my sake, she may let me take the bloom from my wild Ir-ish Rose.

Rose Of Tralee

Words & Music by E. M. Spencer & C.W. Glover
© Copyright 1939 Lawrence Wright Music Company Limited, London WC2.
All Rights Reserved. International Copyright Secured.

Slowly (with feeling)

The pale moon was rising above the green mountain, the sun was declining beneath the blue sea. When I stray'd with my love to the pure crystal

cool shades of ev'ning their mantle were spreading, and Mary all smiling was list'ning to me. The moon through the valley her pale rays was

foun-tain that stands in the beau-ti-ful vale of Tra-lee. She was lovely and
shed-ding, when I won the heart of the rose of Tra-lee. Though

fair as the rose of the sum-mer, yet 'twas not her beau-ty a-lone that won

me, oh, no! 'Twas the truth in her eye ev-er dawn-ing, that made me love

Ma-ry, the rose of Tra-lee. The

Patsy Fagan (The Dacent Irish Boy)

Words & Music by Thomas P. Keenan

© Copyright 1947 Box & Cox Publications Limited, London W1.
All Rights Reserved. International Copyright Secured.

Moderato

VERSE

1. I'm workin' here in Glasgow, I've got a dacent job, carryin' bricks and mortar and me pay is fifteen bob. I

F Dm B♭ F/A Dm F7 B♭ D7 Gm C7
rise up in the morn - in' I get up with the lark, and
CHORUS
F B♭ F/A Dm B♭ B♭m F C7
as I'm walk - in' down the street, you can hear the girls re - mark, "Hel -
F Dm B♭ F C7
lo Pat - sy Fa - gan!" You can hear the girls all cry, "Hel -
F Am B♭ F/A Dm C/G G7 C C7
lo Pat - sy Fa - gan, you're the ap - ple of me eye. You're a
fr3

da - cent boy from Ire - land, there's no one can de - ny, you're a
ra - rem ta - rem di - vil - may ca - rem da - cent Ir - ish boy. Now boy.

rall. last time

Verse 2:
Now if there's one among you
Would like to marry me
I'll take her to a little home
Across the Irish sea.
I'll dress her up in satin
And please her all I can
And let her people see that I'm
A dacent Irishman.

Verse 3:
The day that I left Ireland
'Twas many years ago
I left me home in Antrim
Where the pigs and praties grow.
But since I left old Ireland
It's always been my plan
To let the people see that I'm
A dacent Irishman.

The Spinning Wheel

Words & Music by John Francis Waller & Delia Murphy

© Copyright 1948 Waltons Musical Instrument Galleries (Publication Department) Limited, Dublin.
Box & Cox (Publications) Limited, 2/3 Fitzroy Mews, London W1.
All Rights Reserved. International Copyright Secured.

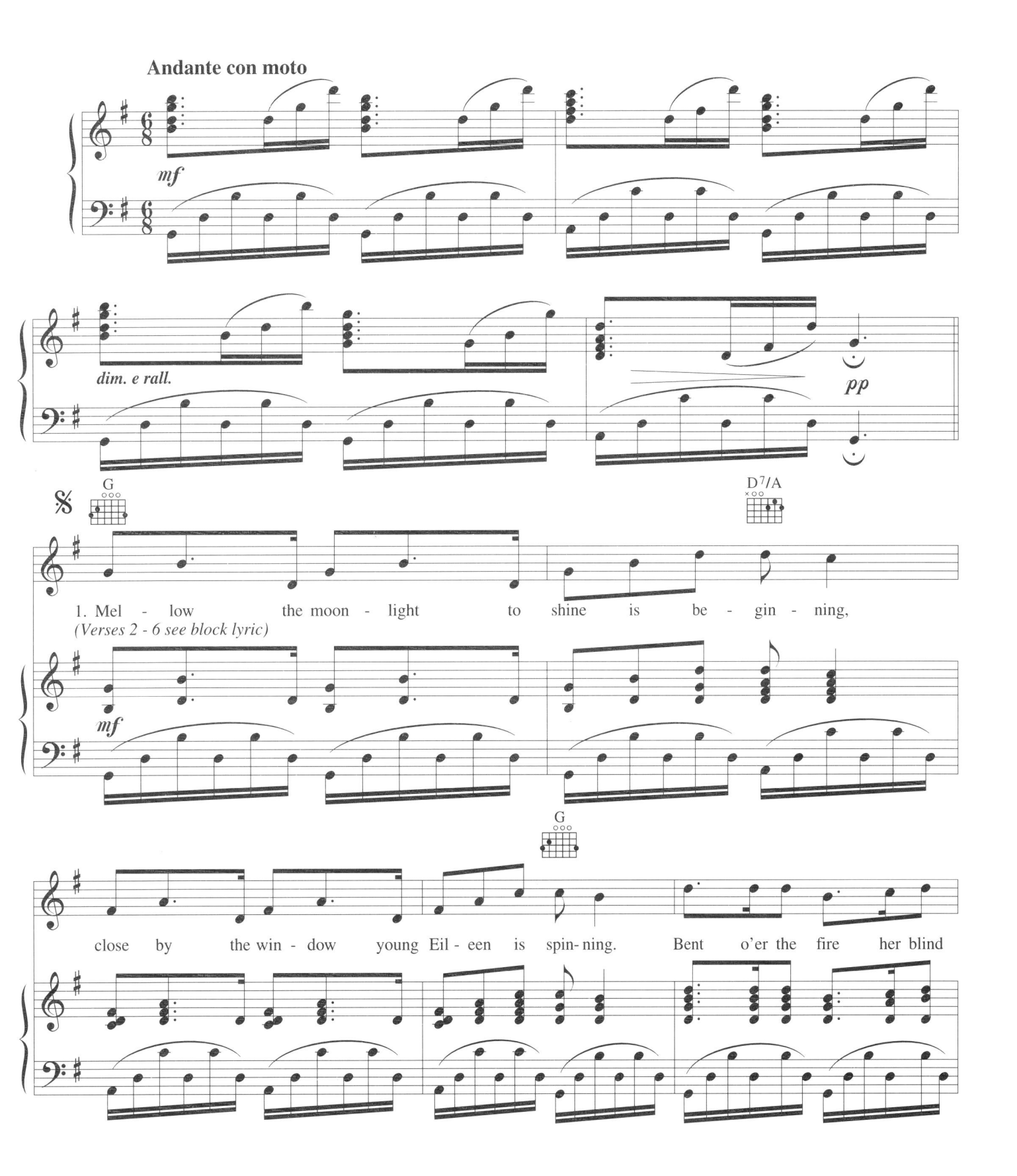

Andante con moto

1. Mellow the moonlight to shine is beginning,
(Verses 2 - 6 see block lyric)
close by the window young Eileen is spinning. Bent o'er the fire her blind

77

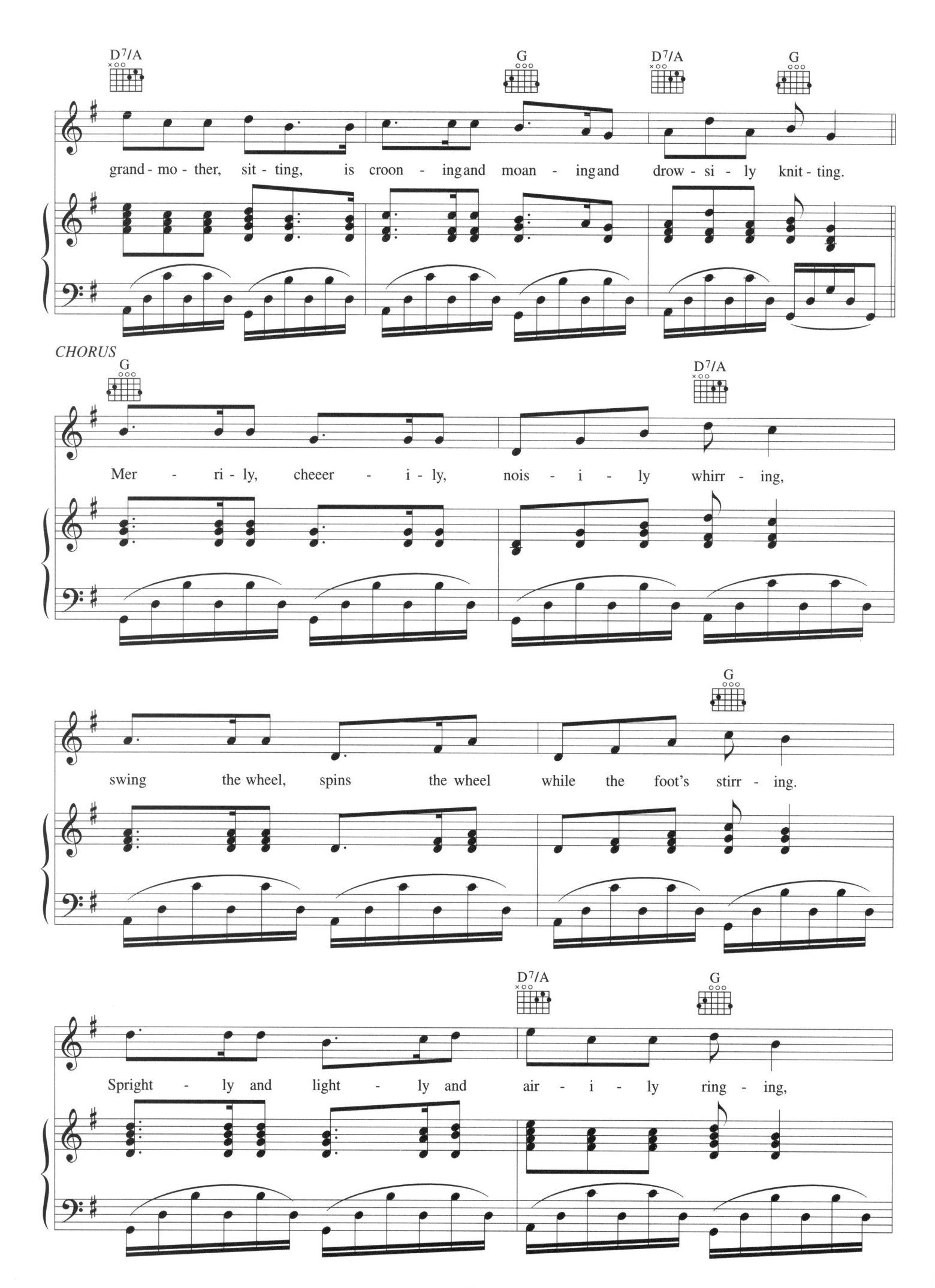

grand-mo-ther, sit-ting, is croon-ing and moan-ing and drow-si-ly knit-ting.

CHORUS

Mer - ri - ly, cheeer - i - ly, nois - i - ly whirr - ing,

swing the wheel, spins the wheel while the foot's stirr - ing.

Spright - ly and light - ly and air - i - ly ring-ing,

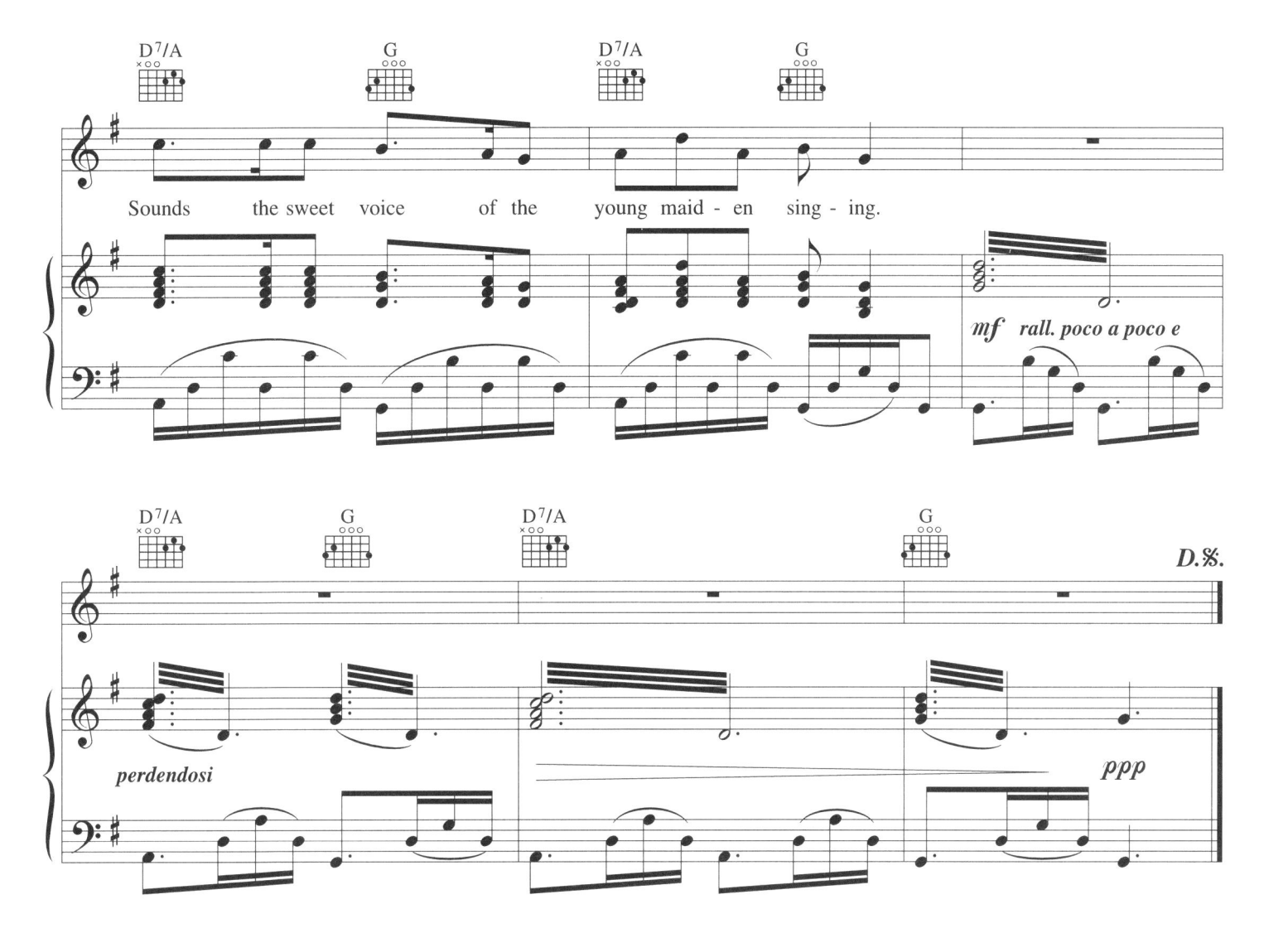

Sounds the sweet voice of the young maid-en sing-ing.

Verse 2:
"Eileen, a chara, I hear someone tapping,"
"'Tis the ivy, dear mother, against the glass flapping,"
"Eily, I surely hear somebody sighing,"
"'Tis the sound, mother dear, of the autumn winds dying,"

Verse 3:
"What's that noise that I hear at the window I wonder?"
"'Tis the little birds chirping the holly-bush under"
"What makes you be pushing and moving your stool on?"
"And singing all wrong the old song of Coolin?"

Verse 4:
There's a form at the casement, the form of her true love,
And he whispers with face bent, "I'm waiting for you, love"
"Get up on the stool, through the lattice step lightly,
And we'll rove in the grove while the moon's shining brightly."

Verse 5:
The maid shakes her head, on her lips lays her fingers,
Steals up from the seat, longs to go and yet lingers,
A frightened glance turns to her drowsy grandmother,
Puts one foot on the stool, spins the wheel with the other.

Verse 6:
Lazily, easily, swings now the wheel round,
Slowly and lowly is heard now the reel's sound,
Noiseless and light to the lattice above her
The maid steps, then leaps to the arms of her lover.

Final Chorus
Slower, and slower, and slower the wheel swings,
Lower, and lower, and lower the reel rings,
Ere the reel and the wheel stopped their spinning and moving,
Through the grove the young lovers by moonlight are roving.

The Town I Loved So Well

Words & Music by Phil Coulter

© Copyright 1980 Four Seasons Music Limited, Killarney House, Killarney Road, Bray, Co. Wicklow, Ireland/Phil Coulter.
All Rights Reserved. International Copyright Secured.

Flowingly with nostalgia

1. In my me-mo-ry ___ I will al-ways ___ see ___ the town that ___ I have ___

(Verses 2, 3, 4 & 5 see block lyric)

loved_____ so well:_____ where our school played ball_____ by the gas yard____ wall_____ and we laughed_____ through the smoke and the smell._____

Go - ing home in the rain_____ run - ning

B♭ D7/A Gm E♭ /D
up the Dark Lane, past the Jail and
Cm F7
down be-hind the Foun-tain, those were
B♭ F/A E♭/G
hap-py days on so ma-ny, ma-ny
B♭ E♭ B♭/F
ways, in the town I loved so

Verse 2:

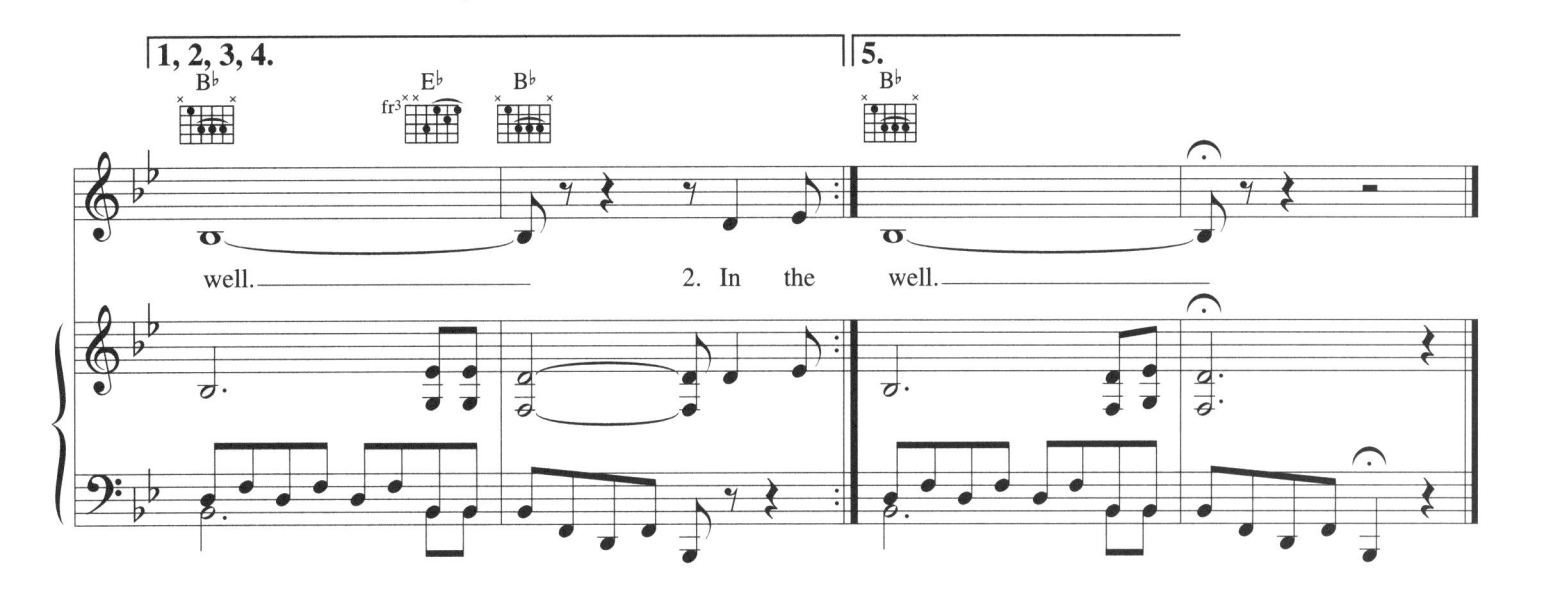

In the early morning the shirt factory horn
Called women from Creggan, the Moor and the Bog
While the men on the dole played a mother's role
Fed the children, and then walked the dog.
And when times got tough, there was just about enough
And they saw it through without complaining
For deep inside was a burning pride
In the town I loved so well.

Verse 3:

There was music there in the Derry air
Like a language that we could all understand
I remember the day that I earned my first pay
When I played in a small pick-up band.
There I spent my youth, and to tell you the truth
I was sad to leave it all behind me
For I'd learned about life and I'd found a wife
In the town I loved so well.

Verse 4:

But when I've returned how my eyes have burned
To see how a town could be brought to its knees
By the armoured cars and the bombed-out bars
And the gas that hangs on to every breeze.
Now the army's installed by that old gas yard wall
And the damned barbed wire gets higher and higher
With their tanks and their guns, oh my God what have they done
To the town I loved so well.

Verse 5:

Now the music's gone but they carry on
For their spirit's been bruised, never broken
They will not forget, but their hearts are set
On tomorrow and peace once again.
For what's done is done, and what's won is won
And what's lost is lost and gone forever
I can only pray for a bright brand new day
In the town I love so well.

When Irish Eyes Are Smiling

Words by George Graff & Chauncey Olcott ♣ Music by Ernest Ball

© Copyright 1912 M. Witmark & Sons, USA.
B. Feldman & Company Limited, 127 Charing Cross Road, London WC2 (75%) &
Redwood Music Limited, Iron Bridge House, 3 Bridge Approach, London NW1 (25%).
All Rights Reserved. International Copyright Secured.

Valse moderato espressivo

1. There's a tear in your eye, and I'm won-der-ing why, for it nev-er should be there at

smile is a part, of the love in your heart, and it makes ev-en sun-shine more

84

all.____ With such pow'r in your smile, sure a stone you'd be-
bright.____ Like the lin-nets sweet song, croon-ing all the day

-guile, so there's nev-er a tear-drop should fall.____ When your
long, comes your laugh-ter so ten-der and light.____ For the

sweet lilt-ing laugh-ter's like some fair-y song, and your eyes twin-kle
spring-time of life is the sweet-est of all, there is ne'er a real

bright as can be.____ You should laugh all the while, and all
care or re-gret.____ And while spring-time is ours through-out

oth - er times smile, and now smile— a smile for me.—
all of youth's hours, let us smile— each chance we get.—

CHORUS
When Ir - ish eyes are smil - ing,— sure it's like a morn - ing spring.— In the lilt of Ir - ish laugh - ter, you can hear the an - gels

G7 C G C
sing. When Ir - ish hearts are hap - py
C7 F C
all the world seems bright and gay. And when
F F♯dim C/G A7 D7
mf porta p
Ir - ish eyes are smil - - - - ing, sure they steal your
mf p
G7 1. C N.C. 2. C F C D.%. al Fine
FINE
heart a - way. When way. 2. For your
f rit.

Whistling Gypsy (The Gypsy Rover)

Words & Music by Leo Maguire

© Copyright 1951 Waltons Musical Instrument Galleries (Publication Department) Limited, Dublin.
Box & Cox (Publications) Limited, 2/3 Fitzroy Mews, London W1.
All Rights Reserved. International Copyright Secured.

Andante moderato

The gyp-sy ro-ver came ov-er the hill, down through the val-ley so sha-dy, he whist-led and sang till the green-woods rang, and he won the heart of a la-dy.

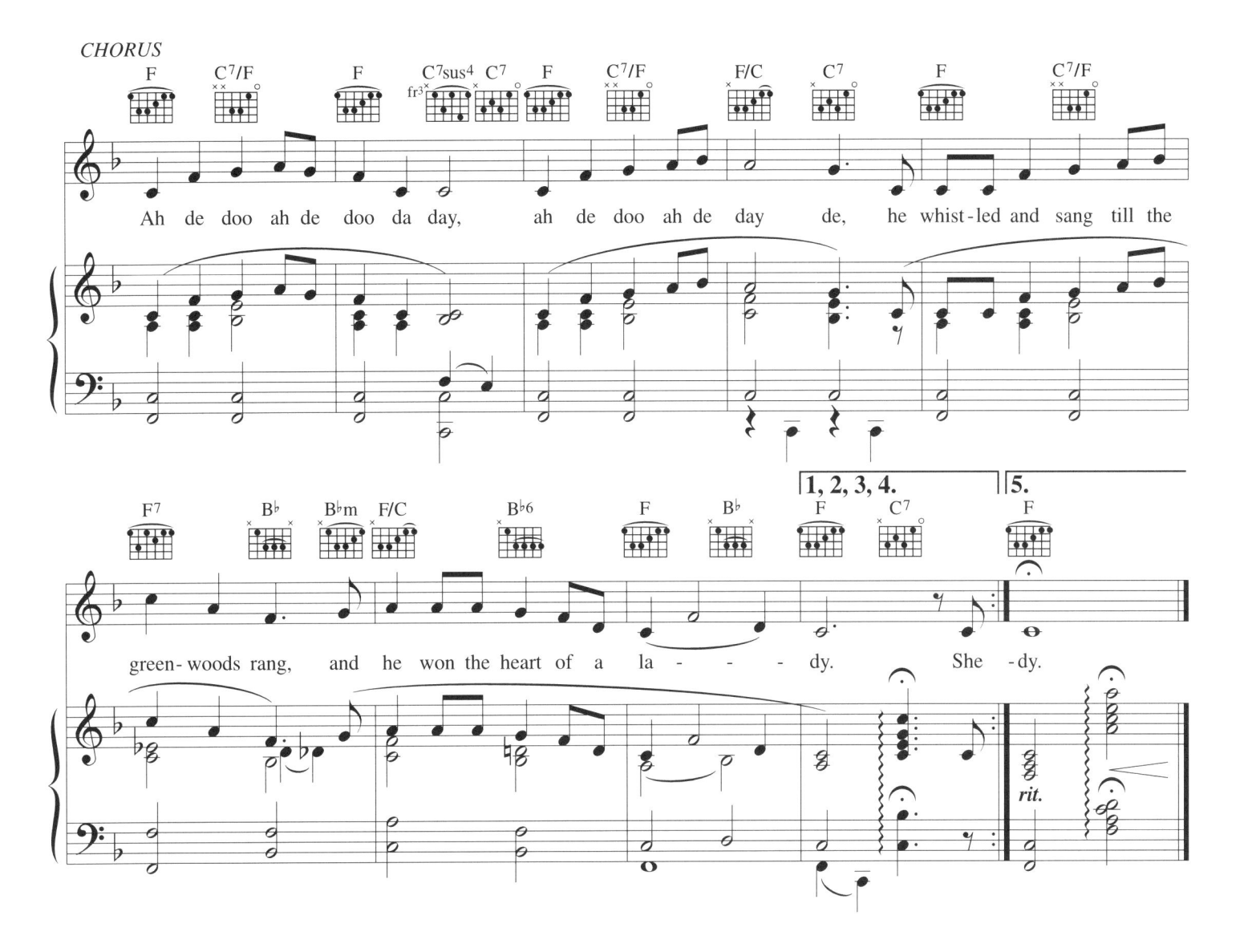

Verse 2:
She left her father's castle gate
She left her fair young lover
She left her servants and her state
To follow the gypsy rover.

Verse 3:
Her father saddled up his fastest steed
He ranged the valleys over
He sought his daughter at great speed
And the whistling gypsy rover.

Verse 4:
He came at last to a mansion fine
Down by the river Clady
And there was music and there was wine
For the gypsy and his lady.

Verse 5:
"He is no gypsy, father dear,
But lord of these lands all over
I'm going to stay 'til my dying day
With my whistling gypsy rover."

The Wild Colonial Boy

Words & Music by Joseph M. Crofts

© Copyright 1950 Walton's Musical Instruments Galleries (Publication Department) Limited, Dublin.
Box & Cox (Publications) Limited, 2/3 Fitzroy Mews, London W1.
All Rights Reserved. International Copyright Secured.

Moderato

1. There was a wild Colonial boy, Jack Dugan was his name, he was born and reared in

(Verses 2-8 see block lyric)

Ireland, in a place called Castlemaine, he was his father's only son and his mother's pride and joy, and dearly did his parents love, the wild colonial

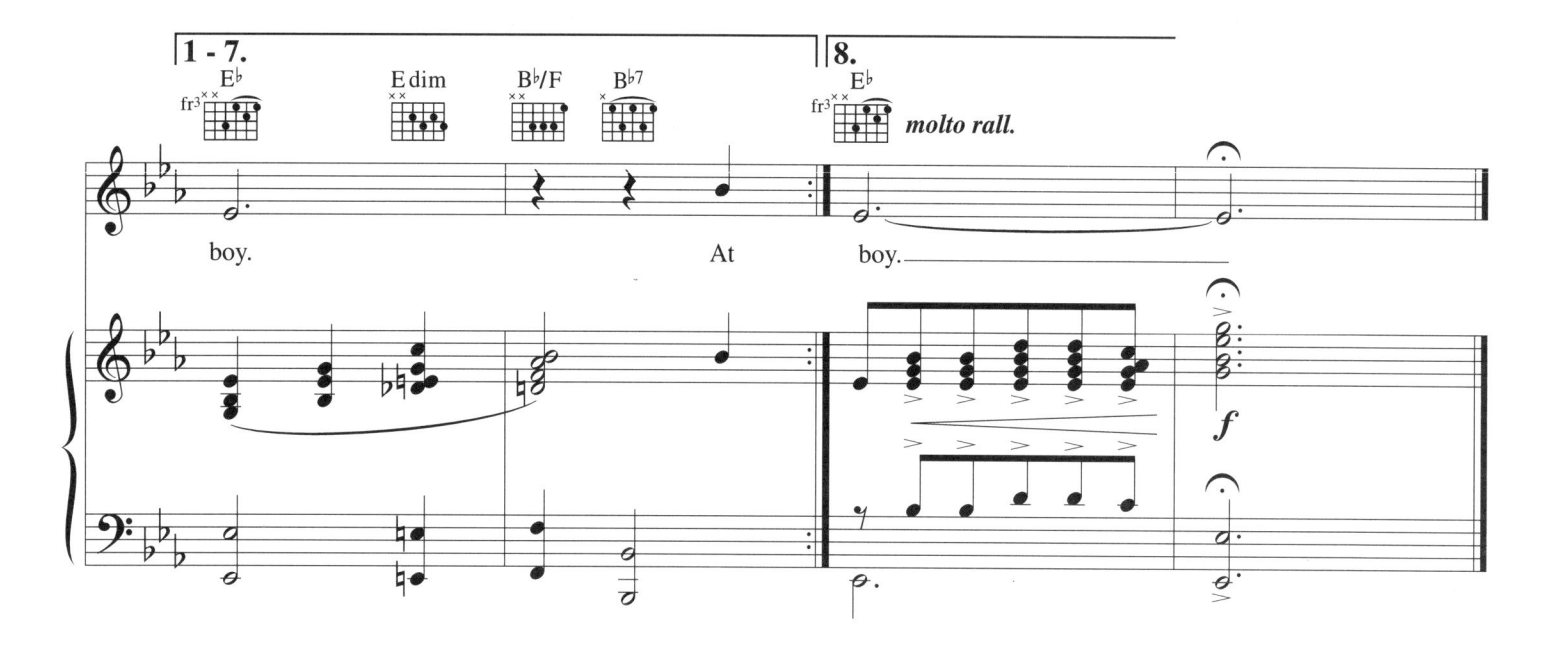

Verse 2:
At hammer throwing Jack was great
Or swinging a Caman
He led the boys in all their pranks
From dusk to early dawn.
At fishin' or at poachin' trout
He was the rale "McCoy"
And all the neighbours loved young Jack
The wild colonial boy.

Verse 3:
At the early age of sixteen years
He left his native home
And to Australia's sunny land
He was inclined to roam.
He robbed the rich, and he helped the poor
He stabbed James MacEvoy
A terror to Australia was
The wild colonial boy.

Verse 4:
For two more years this daring youth
Ran on his wild career
With a head that knew no danger
And a heart that knew no fear.
He robbed outright the wealthy squires
And their arms he did destroy
And woe to all who dared to fight
The wild colonial boy.

Verse 5:
He loved the Prairie and the Bush
Where rangers rode along
With his gun stuck in its holster deep
He sang a merry song.
But if a foe once crossed his track
And sought him to destroy
He'd get sharp shootin' sure from Jack
The wild colonial boy.

Verse 6:
One morning on the Prairie wild
Jack Duggan rode along
While listening to the mocking bird
Singing a cheerful song.
Out jumped three troopers, fierce and grim
Kelly, Davis and Fitzroy
They all set out to capture him
The wild colonial boy.

Verse 7:
"Surrender now, Jack Duggan, come!
You see there's three to one!
Surrender in the Queen's name, sir!
You, are a plundering son!"
Jack drew two pistols from his side
And glared upon Fitzroy,
"I'll fight, but not surrender!" cried
The wild colonial boy.

Verse 8:
He fired a shot at Kelly
Which brought him to the ground
He fired point blank at Davis, too
Who fell dead at the sound.
But a bullet pierced his brave young heart
From the pistol of Fitzroy
And that was how they captured him
The wild colonial boy.

With My Shillelagh Under My Arm

Words & Music by Billy O'Brien & Raymond Wallace

© Copyright 1936 Gordon Cooper and Company. Assigned 1938 Lawrence Wright Music Company Limited, London W1.
All Rights Reserved. International Copyright Secured.

Allegro Moderato *(In a lilting manner)*

Shure, I'm tired of roamin' round and so I'm gonna pack my grip, and I'm off to book my passage on a mighty powerful ship, I'll be bound to send a telegram the

Shure, I'm feelin' mighty fine and I've got bags o' money too, and I mean to give the folks at home a proper Irish do, there'll be such a welcome waitin' for your

93

F Fm/A♭ C/G C/E F C/G
day I reach the quay, just to tell them in a week or two they'll be ex-pect-in'
hum-ble on the mat, I can just i-ma-gine peo-ple say-in' "Och how are ye,
G7 C G7 C F
me. Pat?" With my shil-le-lagh un-der my arm and a twin-kle in my
p-f fz
C F C/E Am D9 D9(♭5) G7
fr4 fr4
eye, I'll be off to Tip-per-ar-y in the morn-in', with my shil-
C G7 C E7aug E7 F C F
le-lagh un-der my arm and a "Too-la-roo-la-li," I'll be wel-come in the
fz

home that I was born in. My mother's told the neighbours that I'm gonna settle down, Phil the Fluter's comin' out to play me round the town, with my shillelagh under my arm and a twinkle in my eye I'll be off to Tipperary in the mornin'. in'.

Exclusive Distributors:

Music Sales Limited
8/9 Frith Street,
London W1V 5TZ, England.

Music Sales Pty Limited
120 Rothschild Avenue,
Rosebery, NSW 2018,
Australia.

Order No. AM951632
ISBN 0-7119-7132-3
This book © Copyright 1998 by Wise Publications

Unauthorised reproduction of any part of this publication by any means
including photocopying is an infringement of copyright.

Book design by Chloë Alexander
Compiled by Peter Evans
Music edited by Paul Honey
Music processed by Paul Ewers Music Design

Printed in the United Kingdom by
Printwise (Haverhill) Limited, Haverhill, Suffolk.

Your Guarantee of Quality
As publishers, we strive to produce every book to the highest
commercial standards.
The music has been freshly engraved and the book has been carefully designed
to minimise awkward page turns and to make playing from it a real pleasure.
Particular care has been given to specifying acid-free, neutral-sized paper
made from pulps which have not been elemental chlorine bleached.
This pulp is from farmed sustainable forests and was produced with special
regard for the environment.
Throughout, the printing and binding have been planned to ensure a sturdy,
attractive publication which should give years of enjoyment.
If your copy fails to meet our high standards, please inform us
and we will gladly replace it.

Music Sales' complete catalogue describes thousands of titles and is available
in full colour sections by subject, direct from Music Sales Limited. Please state
your areas of interest and send a cheque/postal order for £1.50 for postage to:
Music Sales Limited, Newmarket Road, Bury St. Edmunds, Suffolk IP33 3YB.